# A Thousand Peaks

## Poems from China

by Siyu Liu and Orel Protopopescu

Illustrated by Siyu Liu

Pacific View Press
Berkeley, California

*To Iris and Spring*

Thank you, Bo, for your technical support. Thank you, Orel, for your poetic translations and perseverance.
—*Siyu Liu*

*To Xenia and Nuria*

Thank you, Siyu, for approaching me with this idea. Our collaboration has been a joy. Thanks to Serban for his constant support, and to the members of my writing group for insight and friendship.
—*Orel Protopopescu*

## Acknowledgements

The authors wish to thank Pam Zumwalt, Bob Schildgen, and Nancy Ippolito, our editors, for their faith in our work and their contributions to its realization. Thanks to Sandy Lanton, who helped us find the best publisher for this project, and to Min-Huei Lu, librarian at SUNY, Stony Brook, who generously assisted our research.

Pacific View Press would like to thank Jeannette Faurot for her careful reading of the manuscript and sound advice and Ma Baolin for proofreading the Chinese text. Special thanks to Jos Sances, Robbin Henderson, and Dina Redman who gave generously of their time and provided invaluable design insights and inspiration.

Text copyright © 2002 Orel Protopopescu and Siyu Liu

Translation © 2002 Orel Protopopescu and Siyu Liu

Illustrations copyright © 2002 Siyu Liu

Cover design by Siyu Liu

Library of Congress Catalog Card Number: 2001034008

ISBN 1-881896-24-2

Printed in China by Global Interprint, Inc.

Library of Congress Cataloging-in-Publication Data

Liu, Siyu, 1964-
    A thousand peaks : poems from China / Siyu Liu and Orel Protopopescu ; illustrated by Siyu Liu
        p. cm.
    Includes bibliographical references and index.
    Summary: A collection of thirty-five poems spanning nineteen centuries, representing both famous and lesser-known poets, including both the Chinese text and a literal translation.
        ISBN 1-881896-24-2
    1. Chinese poetry--Translations into English--Juvenile literature. [1. Chinese poetry--Collections.] I. Protopopescu, Orel Odinov. II. Title
PL2658.E3 L59 2001
895.1'152--dc21

2001034008

# Contents

# Introduction

IN CHINA, POETRY BEGAN OVER FIVE THOUSAND YEARS AGO. The first poems were songs. At festivals and other important events, people composed new lyrics to go with familiar tunes. They sang their thoughts and feelings to each other. Court musicians sang during official government meetings to help politicians negotiate. Imagine songwriters singing in Congress today! The first known collection of the ancient poems, the *Book of Songs,* was written on bamboo sticks around 600 B.C.E.

Court musicians studied the peoples' songs, which often spoke of problems with court officials, to advise the kings on how well they were doing. These musicians were the pollsters of their day. The scholar and teacher, Confucius (551–479 B.C.E.) insisted his son learn the songs so he would be fit for educated society. After the time of Confucius, poetry started to separate from music.

These were times of great upheaval. Seven small kingdoms constantly fought with each other. In 221 B.C.E. the king of one conquered all the others. He named his regime the Qin dynasty and gave himself the title Qin Shihuang, which means "first emperor of Qin." The name China comes from *Qin,* pronounced *chin.*

Qin Shihuang was clever and ruthless. Thousands of laborers lost their lives constructing his palace, his vast underground tomb, and the Great Wall he ordered built to protect his empire from invaders. He had almost all books destroyed, so he could not be compared unfavorably with past rulers. Some books were hidden and saved, but the *Book of Music,* which had accompanied the *Book of Songs,* disappeared forever. Qin forced all the states to adopt one written language. Although many dialects are still spoken in China, because of Qin Shihuang everyone uses the same Chinese characters.

The first emperor had claimed his dynasty would last forever, but eventually the people rebelled. The Qin dynasty was over by 206 B.C.E., when the Han dynasty began. During the Han dynasty, a style of poetry, *shi* (the Chinese word for poetry) emerged that has lasted to this day. *Shi* poems in their simplest form have five or seven characters per line and four or eight lines per poem. The second and fourth lines usually rhyme, and sometimes the first line rhymes too. A typical poem often uses the first two lines to paint a picture, the third to offer a twist, a new angle on the subject, and the last to reflect the poet's thoughts. This may include advice for the listener. All the poems in this book are *shi* poems, and they show the remarkable consistency of the form from the Han era to the 20th century.

The art of poetry reached a new high point during the Tang dynasty (618–907). These were prosperous times, with ideas flowing into and out of the country. Block printing was invented, which made publishing easier. Every educated man was required to learn poetry. A collection of the times, *All the Poems of the Tang Dynasty*, included 40,000 poems.

Emperor Wu Zetian, a woman who ruled from 684 to 704, added poems composed in the *shi* style to the qualifying exams for government jobs. Poetry was excluded from these exams at the end of the Song dynasty (960–1279), but poems, especially those later collected in *Three Hundred Poems of the Tang Dynasty*, were still taught to children. They often memorized these poems before they knew how to read.

POETRY CONTESTS WERE POPULAR. Family members or friends would compose a poem on the same subject in the same style. Or they might have a matching contest. They gathered together in a circle, selected a topic and style, and drew lots to see who would start the verse. Each player had to come up with a line to match the previous one. Whoever couldn't create a matching line would have to sip wine. At the end of the contest, everyone could see who had lost!

Although women were allowed to participate in these contests, their poems seldom traveled outside family circles. Only the most memorable works of a few women poets survive today. An old Chinese saying states, "A woman of no talent is a woman of virtue." An ordinary woman in ancient China was not expected to think. She was supposed to serve her family before she married, her husband after she married, and her sons if her husband died before her. Women of noble families were educated, but were seldom allowed to leave the family quarters. Only unusual families celebrated a daughter's talents.

While many people throughout China's history composed poems, those recorded and passed down to us were most often written by members of the educated ruling class. Today, men and women of all backgrounds compose poems. For festivals, weddings, or other important events, poets are asked to write lucky couplets, two-line poems. Sometimes people copy lines from classical poems onto red paper, and hang one line on either side of a doorway. Red, in China, is the color of good luck. Chinese people still believe that without poetry a person can't become his or her best self.

# Pity the Farmer

## Social Structure

A DYNASTY'S SURVIVAL DEPENDED ON HOW EMPERORS TREATED THEIR SUBJECTS. Most Chinese were farmers. Their social rank was below officials but higher than craftsmen, artisans, and merchants. Emperors called on the farmers to defend the country and to build palaces, canals, roads, and other projects, such as the Great Wall. If the farmers were heavily taxed, drafted too often into the army, or spent too much time building, a terrible food shortage could follow, and then they might rebel. Many dynasties were weakened and even destroyed by peasant rebellions.

Peasant women raised silkworms and wove the silk that made the Chinese empire rich. Chinese silk was soft, delicate, and in demand. No one knows when the ancient caravans started, but the Chinese were sending silk over the first Silk Road all the way to Rome by the first century B.C.E. These caravans traveled through barren mountains and the Gobi Desert to buy the precious silk. Silk brought in big profits. In order to keep the trade going, peace treaties with neighboring countries became very important. The fiercest neighbors, who lived north of China, frequently raided the border cities on horses, despite the Great Wall. Many lives were lost in battle. In order to avoid more death and expense, an emperor would sometimes marry his daughters or his concubines to the kings of neighboring countries. This was a way of buying peace, for a time.

Although useful in political marriages, daughters did not have the same value as sons. By tradition, a girl after marriage would live with her in-laws, and was considered their property. She couldn't inherit anything and was expected to take care of her in-laws. A son would stay home, inherit what his father left him, produce sons to carry on the family name, and take care of his aging parents. Wives who couldn't produce sons lacked respect in the family. Poor parents, who depended on someone to take care of them in old age, often considered raising a daughter a waste of time and money.

Until 1949, a man could have as many wives as he could afford. However, the first wife's oldest son usually inherited the property. The first marriage was often arranged between families of suitable rank. Concubines were bought from less affluent families. An emperor might have hundreds of concubines. His followers, eager to please, sought out the most beautiful and gifted girls, and gave them to him. A few, the emperor's favorites, acquired the title of imperial concubine.

When an emperor died, the throne usually passed to the empress's oldest son. But sometimes there were bitter power struggles between sons, court officials, the empress, and the emperor's other wives. After a few years or several hundred, a dynasty would weaken, and be overthrown. A new leader (native or invader) would declare himself emperor and set up a new dynasty.

Though it was hard for lower-class individuals to move up in society, it was not impossible. Many men from humble families entered government service through the exam system. They could work their way up to become high imperial officials.

# Pity the Farmer

In the noonday sun, he hoes his grain,
his sweat watering the plants like rain.
Who knows, maybe the food on your plate
comes, every grain, from his toil and strain?

by LI SHEN (Tang dynasty)

For centuries, this poem has been used to teach Chinese children to appreciate other people's work and not waste food.

Li Shen lived in the late Tang dynasty, a time of instability. During his life, three different emperors held power. Upheaval at court, rebellions, and invasions upset the farmers' routine. They had to leave their fields to fight for the emperor. Invading armies often stole or destroyed their crops. To support themselves, some peasants became thieves, holding up travelers.

Legend says Li was once captured by bandits. The chief, who knew him by name, called for a sample of his art on the spot. Li composed a poem saying there was no reason to fear highwaymen, as more than half the world contained more dangerous men. He promptly won his release.

The last line in Chinese repeats the word *grain* to emphasize its value. This doubling, used for emphasis and to create a balanced sound, is a common feature of Chinese poetry.

mǐn nóng
悯 农
pity farmer

chú hé rì dāng wǔ
锄 禾 日 当 午
hoe grain sun at noon

hàn dī hé xià tǔ
汗 滴 禾 下 土
sweat drop grain below earth

shuí zhī pán zhōng cān
谁 知 盘 中 餐
who know plate middle meal

lì lì jiē xīn kǔ
粒 粒 皆 辛 苦
grain grain all hard labor

李 绅

# Passing Huaqing Palace

From a distance, Changan is a heap of embroidery.
A thousand doors lead into the mountain palace.
A concubine smiles down at the rider's red dust,
for who could guess litchis get urgent delivery?

by Du Mu (803–852, Tang dynasty)

guò huá qīng gōng jué jù
过 华 清 宫 绝 句
pass Huaqing Palace
ruled poem

cháng ān huí wàng xiù
chéng duī
长 安 回 望 绣 成 堆
Changan turn look
embroidery become pile

shān dǐng qiān mén cì dì kāi
山 顶 千 门 次 地 开
mountain top thousand
door in sequence open

yí jì hóng chén fēi zǐ xiào
一 骑 红 尘 妃 子 笑
one rider red dust imperial
concubine smile

wú rén zhī shì lì zhī lái
无 人 知 是 荔 枝 来
no body know is litchi
come

杜 牧

The Tang emperors built their palace, Huaqing, on the beautiful Mount Li, outside their capital, Changan, today's Xian. From its mountaintop perch, the imperial rulers looked down on their subjects below.

The Tang emperor, Xuan Zong, enjoyed an easy rule for 40 years. Then he fell in love with a beautiful woman, Yang Yuhuan, whom he named Precious Imperial Concubine. To make her happy, he let her brother become his premier. To have more time for her, he put his adopted son, An Lushan, in charge of the army. To keep her smiling, he ordered his imperial riders to deliver litchis, a tropical fruit, from China's far south.

An Lushan rebelled and led the army against the emperor, who fled with Yang. But the emperor's guards demanded the lives of Yang and her brother in return for their continued loyalty. The emperor finally gave in, but his tears flowed like rain.

An official whose grandfather was a premier, Du Mu dared to criticize the court he served. In this poem he described the extravagant way of life that many believed caused Xuan Zong's downfall. Was he sending a signal to his own emperor?

# *Clouds*

They show ten thousand shapes, but not a drop of rain,
mirror themselves in water, pile up on a mountain chain.
As far as you can see, seedlings wither and die
while clouds pretend to be strange peaks in an idle sky.

by LAI HU (Tang dynasty)

Although An Lushan's revolt was crushed, the Tang empire was seriously weakened. The next hundred years were filled with foreign invasions, peasant uprisings, and power struggles among local and military leaders. Caught in between these factions, the peasants' lives were miserable.

Officials collected taxes and forced peasants into government service. Corrupt officials used these workers to enrich themselves. Like the weather, their behavior greatly affected people's lives. The double meaning of this poem is clear: Government officials were often useless and cruel, indifferent as clouds that won't rain.

This poem is a classic seven-character-per-line *shi*. The first two lines present a vivid picture of clouds in the sky. The third line suddenly changes the angle of vision to take in the thirsty seedlings. They represent the farmers, watching the clouds, hoping for rain. The final line shows the poet's point of view, full of sympathy for the farmers and contempt for the officials.

Confucius once said, "If the poems of a country are mostly sad, it is the signal of its ending."

yún
云
cloud

qiān xíng wàn xiàng jìng huán kōng
千 形 万 象 竟 还 空
thousand shape ten thousand image actually still useless

yìng shuǐ cáng shān piàn fù chóng
映 水 藏 山 片 复 重
reflect water hide mountain piece again overlap

wú xiàn hàn miáo kū yù jìn
无 限 旱 苗 枯 欲 尽
no boundary drought seedling wither about die

yōu yōu xián chù zuò qí fēng
悠 悠 闲 处 作 奇 峰
leisurely leisurely idle place pretend strange peak

来 鹄

# Chrysanthemum Song

Rustling in the west wind, you fill the yard,
but your freezing scent lures few butterflies.
One day, I'll let you bloom with peach blossoms,
if I grow up to be god of the skies.

by HUANG CHAO (?–884, Tang dynasty)

fù jú huā
赋 菊 花
chant chrysanthemum
blossom

sà sà xī fēng mǎn yuàn zāi
飒 飒 西 风 满 院 栽
rustle rustle west wind fill
yard plant

ruǐ hán xiāng lěng dié nán
lái
蕊 寒 香 冷 蝶 难 来
stamen cold fragrance
freezing butterfly difficult
come

tā nián wǒ ruò wéi qīng dì
他 年 我 若 为 青 帝
future year I if become
sky god

bào yǔ táo huā yí chù kāi
报 与 桃 花 一 处 开
declare let peach blossom
one place bloom

黄 巢

A series of incompetent emperors ruled China during the last few decades of the Tang dynasty. Corruption, from the top down, weakened the empire.

When Huang Chao was five years old, his father and grandfather were having a poetry contest on the theme of chrysanthemums, flowers that bloom in autumn. Huang Chao interrupted with a line of his own. His father was annoyed with his rude behavior and wanted to spank him. His grandfather, however, forgave him and let him continue until he came up with this poem.

After Huang grew up, he saw no future for himself in this dying dynasty. He joined dissatisfied farmers, leading them in a takeover of the capital city, Changan. The emperor fled. Huang established his own dynasty, Qi, in 880. His troops robbed and killed the rich, especially the Tang officials, in the name of the poor. The capital was in chaos, and Huang lost public support. The emperor fought back, and Huang was executed in 884.

Peasant rebellions continued to weaken the dynasty. By 907, the Tang dynasty, after ruling for 300 years, ended. China entered a period of turmoil.

# Poem of My Lost Country

My lord raised a flag of surrender over his walled town.
Buried deep in his palace, what could I know of it then?
A hundred and forty thousand men put their weapons down.
How shocking to find not one man among them!

by LADY HUARUI (Tang dynasty)

In 960, the warlord Zhao Kuangyin claimed the throne and established the Song dynasty. Soon after, he began conquering the small kingdoms that threatened his rule. The King of Shu in today's Sichuan province couldn't hold off the imperial army and, in 965, he walked out of his fortress and surrendered.

Lady Huarui, his talented and beautiful concubine, was blamed for distracting him and causing his failure. Having heard of her talents, the Song emperor ordered her and the king to his capital, Kaifeng, in Henan province.

After the King of Shu died, the emperor, captivated by Lady Huarui, made her his own concubine. One day, he asked her for a poem. She defended her reputation by writing the verse above.

Lady Huarui painted her first husband, the King of Shu, dressed in purple holding a slingshot. She told the emperor this character was a god who would send children to women who worshipped him. Soon everyone in the palace had the painting copied and hung in their bedrooms! The emperor's brother, suspicious of Lady Huarui, warned the emperor that she might murder him to avenge her first husband's fall from power. Some say this brother killed Lady Huarui on a hunting trip, pretending it was an accident.

14

shù guó wáng shī
述 国 亡 诗
tell country dead poem

jūn wáng chéng shàng shù xiáng qí
君 王 城 上 竖 降 旗
majesty king city top erect surrender flag

qiè zài shēn gōng nǎ dé zhī
妾 在 深 宫 那 得 知
I stay deep palace how can know

shí sì wàn rén qí xiè jiǎ
十 四 万 人 齐 解 甲
fourteen ten thousand people all remove armor

nìng wú yí gè shì nán ér
宁 无 一 个 是 男 儿
how not one is male

花 蕊 夫 人

# Presented to Premier Kou

For one clear song you gave a bolt of silk,
yet still the beauty felt her payment slight.
She didn't know how many times the weaver
cast a shuttle in dim windowlight.

by QIAN TAO (Song dynasty)

chéng kòu gōng
呈 寇 公
present Kou Premier

yì qǔ qīng gē yí shù líng
一 曲 清 歌 一 束 绫
one piece clear song one bolt silk

měi rén yóu zì yì xián qīng
美 人 犹 自 意 嫌 轻
beautiful person still feel resent light

bù zhī zhī nǚ yíng chuāng xià
不 知 织 女 萤 窗 下
not know weave woman firefly window under

jǐ dù pāo suō zhī dé chéng
几 度 抛 梭 织 得 成
how many cast shuttle weave make complete

茜 桃

For common people, the Song dynasty was not much better than the Tang. They worked to produce wealth for the court and nobles.

Qian Tao was a concubine/servant (the lowest grade of concubine) of an important minister in the Song government, Premier Kou (962–1023). One day, a famous singer came to their house. The premier listened while drinking from a golden cup. After several songs, Premier Kou gave the singer a bolt of fine quality silk. The beautiful singing girl was not satisfied. Qian Tao saw this incident and composed two poems to present to Premier Kou. The one above is the first. She wanted to call his attention to the contrast between the lavish life of the court and the hardships of the peasants. After Kou read the poems, he wrote his own:

*What comes of premiers and all famous names?*
*They pass like running shuttles, changing scenes.*
*Don't ask about the world's endless wrongs.*
*Let's drink and listen to gorgeous songs.*

15

# Poem in Seven Paces

Beanstalks burn to boil beans though
beans cry out from the pot:
We come from the same roots, you know.
Why rush to torture each other so?

by CAO ZHI (192–232, Han dynasty)

Long before the Song dynasty, power struggles dominated court life.

Cao Cao, a premier of the Han dynasty, wanted to overthrow the emperor and establish a dynasty of his own. He diminished the Han emperor's power until the emperor had no real authority. When Cao Cao had to select his successor among his two sons, Cao Pi and Cao Zhi, he tested both of them for their talents, wisdom, and courage. Although his favorite son, Cao Zhi, was more talented in art, music and literature, he was weak and frivolous. Cao Cao groomed Cao Pi to succeed him. Cao Pi, upon his father's death, declared himself the emperor of a new kingdom, Wei (220–265), finally realizing his father's dream.

According to legend, Cao Pi wanted to get rid of Cao Zhi and ordered him to compose a poem before he had taken seven steps, or die. The result, this poem, saved his life. It vividly portrays the brothers' tortured relationship.

This poem is a classic five-character-per-line *shi*. The first two lines show the beans cooking over burning beanstalks. The third line changes the point of view, showing the relationship between the beans and the beanstalks, which symbolize the two brothers. The final line is the poet's plea for his brother's compassion.

qī bù shī
七 步 诗
seven pace poem

zhǔ dòu rán dòu qí
煮 豆 燃 豆 其
boil bean burn bean stalk

dòu zài fǔ zhōng qì
豆 在 釜 中 泣
bean in pot middle cry

běn shì tóng gēn shēng
本 是 同 根 生
actually is same root born

xiāng jiān hé tài jí
相 煎 何 太 急
mutually fry why much hurry

曹 植

16

# Clothes Made of Gold Thread

Don't value clothes made of gold thread,
Sir, please value your youth instead.
Break branches in bloom while you can,
Sir, don't wait till the flowers are dead.

by DU QIUNIANG (Tang dynasty)

jīn lǚ yī
金 缕 衣
golden thread garment

quàn jūn mò xī jīn lǚ yī
劝 君 莫 惜 金 缕 衣
urge sir don't value
golden thread garment

quàn jūn xī qǔ shào nián shí
劝 君 惜 取 少 年 时
urge sir value take young
year time

huā kāi kān zhé zhí xǔ zhé
花 开 勘 折 直 许 折
flower bloom can break
just permit break

mò dài wú huā kōng zhé zhī
莫 待 无 花 空 折 枝
don't wait no blossom
only break twig

杜 秋 娘

Power struggles over succession not only affected the imperial rulers, but also those who depended on them.

Du Qiuniang was taken as a concubine by the Tang emperor Xian Zong after her husband rebelled and was killed by the emperor's army. The poet Du Mu saw Du Qiuniang dancing and singing at the palace. He was amazed by her talents when she sang this poem to her own tune.

After Xian Zong died, his son, Mu Zong, named Qiuniang "Teaching Mother" to one of the princes, in charge of supervising his studies. When the prince grew older, he received the title of King Zhang.

However, when Mu Zong died, another prince who was King Zhang's brother inherited the throne. Feeling threatened, he deposed King Zhang. Du Qiuniang was ordered to return to her hometown. Du Mu found her there and recorded her life in a long poem called the *Ballad of Qiuniang*.

While writing the lines above, perhaps Qiuniang realized how fragile her own situation was, dependent on powerful men.

# Song of a Tung Tree by a Well

In the yard is an ancient tung tree
whose trunk climbs through the clouds.
Branches welcome birds from north and south.
Leaves wave to winds moving in and out.

by XUE TAO (770–832, Tang dynasty)

Xue Tao, one of the Tang dynasty's most famous woman poets, was luckier than Qiuniang. Born in Changan, she followed her father south to his official post, in Sichuan.

Xue began to compose poems when she was only seven. One day, her father pointed to a tung tree and made up the first two lines of this poem. Xue Tao met his challenge by creating the last two lines. Her father was so impressed he was speechless. Yet he feared the poem was a bad omen, that it meant his daughter's life would be spent serving others.

After her father died, Xue became a musician. She served wine, composed poems, and sang for the nobles. An official, Wei Gao, admired her talent. He tried to obtain for her the post of "official secretary," but failed. However, he often asked her for advice on political decisions. Later, Xue worked for other officials in Sichuan.

She also invented a pine-needle-patterned, dark-red paper that became fashionable for letter writing. When she retired, she became a Daoist priestess, living in isolation in a little house built with her own funds. In a poem she wrote, "Like a general, a beauty shouldn't let the world see her gray hair."

jǐng wú yín
井 梧 吟
well tung-tree chant

tíng chú yì gǔ tóng
庭 除 一 古 桐
yard only one ancient tung

sǒng gàn rù yún zhōng
耸 干 入 云 中
towering trunk enter cloud middle

zhī yíng nán běi niǎo
枝 迎 南 北 鸟
branch welcome south north bird

yè sòng wǎng lái fēng
叶 送 往 来 风
leaf see-off go come wind

薛 涛

# Traveling in Long Xi

Swearing to wipe out Huns, they forgot their lives,
five thousand fur-clad men, lost in barbarian dust.
Pity their bones by the Wu Ding's riverside,
still walking through the spring dreams of their wives.

by CHEN TAO (Tang dynasty)

lǒng xī xíng
陇 西 行
Long Xi travel

shì sǎo xiōng nú bú gù shēn
誓 扫 匈 奴 不 顾 身
swear sweep Hun not
worry self

wǔ qiān diāo jǐn sàng hú
chén
五 千 貂 锦 丧 胡 尘
five thousand marten
brocade lost barbarian
dust

kě lián wú dìng hé biān gǔ
可 怜 无 定 河 边 骨
pity Mu Ding River side
bone

yóu shì chūn guī mèng lǐ
rén
犹 是 春 闺 梦 里 人
still is spring harem
dream inside person

陈 陶

In ancient times, the Chinese people fought frequently with nomads from the northwest. One group, the Huns, were fierce enemies. Swift with their horses and swords, they raided Chinese cities along the border. They came and went as they pleased and didn't seem interested in leading a settled life.

Several times northerners conquered China. The Han majority considered those times of shame, but in some ways China benefitted. During the Mongols' rule, the Yuan dynasty (1279–1368), Chinese merchants grew rich from the silk, tea, and porcelain sent to Central Asia and Europe over the now-peaceful Silk Road. The Manchus, who established China's last dynasty, the Qing, in 1644, added vast lands to China's territory.

19

# Passing the Jinshi Exam

## Scholar-Officials

CHINESE EMPERORS REALIZED THEY NEEDED MANY TRUSTWORTHY OFFICIALS to carry out their orders and report information. To hire only the emperor's relatives and friends would create chaos. The conflicts among these people could soon end an emperor's dynasty. How could an emperor who seldom ventured outside his palace find qualified candidates?

Before the first dynasty was established, the kings of the many states that formed ancient China selected heirs to their thrones according to merit. The heirs were not necessarily the king's own sons. The best candidate had to be someone honest, kind, generous, and wise. During the Han dynasty, the local governments recommended qualified candidates to advise the emperor. The Sui emperors (581–618) who reorganized China after 300 years of disruption, introduced the *jinshi* (advanced scholar) examination to test the skills of potential officials. The Tang dynasty perfected the system.

The *jinshi* exam tested a man's understanding about how to govern a country. The man who passed this difficult exam would be a candidate for an official post (job). The posts had nine levels and a man would be assigned to one according to his score. Women were not allowed to take the exam, nor were people whose occupations were unworthy, such as actors and shop owners.

Poetry was part of the *jinshi* exams until a Song dynasty reformer, Wang Anshi, claimed that the exam should find the best officials, not poets. During the Tang dynasty, a candidate could also take exams designed for particular talents, such as history or math. After the Ming dynasty (1368–1644), the *jinshi* exams tested only classics by Confucius and other sages.

Confucius was a Zhou-era scholar-official. Born a commoner, he rose to a high government position, but resigned to protest his prince's misrule. He spent years wandering and teaching, searching for a ruler worthy of his service. His teachings on social order were later officially adopted by Han dynasty emperors and shaped Chinese society for over 2,000 years.

An ambitious Chinese man aspired to the Confucian ideal that required him to serve the emperor and state. If he couldn't pass the *jinshi* exam, he usually couldn't obtain a post to prove himself. If a man passed the *jinshi* exam, he would bring honor, fortune, fame, and power to his family. The posts often required the successful candidate to move away from his home town. Many felt guilty leaving their families behind. Ironically, the Confucian ideal of filial piety required a man to live with his family and tend to his parents.

The political world was hostile. An official could lose his freedom of speech for merely hinting at his political views in his poems. One who resisted political pressure would not get a good job. Officials could be caught up in conspiracies that failed. Outcasts were often sent to remote posts, exiled, or even executed.

By the 19th century, the *jinshi* exam was out-of-date. It didn't test math and science. Forced into studies they considered useless, many Chinese scholar-officials felt poorly prepared for the modern world. The *jinshi* exam was abandoned in 1906, just five years before the collapse of China's last dynasty.

# Passing the Jinshi Exam

My past life held no praiseworthy hours,
but now my thoughts have infinite powers.
My horse, triumphant, gallops in spring winds.
In one day, I've seen all of Changan's flowers.

by MENG JIAO (751–814, Tang dynasty)

A Chinese idiom, "to look at flowers while galloping" means to browse quickly without noticing any details. It probably came from this ancient poem.

The poet, Meng Jiao, was eccentric and lived like a hermit in his early years. He decided to take the *jinshi* exam when he was 41, but failed badly. When he finally passed it, a decade later, his joy didn't last. Bored by his trivial job, he asked his underlings to impersonate him and share his salary. He preferred to earn less and have more time to write poetry. He was soon fired and spent the rest of his years living off his friends and a few powerful patrons.

dēng kē hòu
登 科 后
pass *jinshi* exam

xī rì wò chuò bù zú kuā
昔 日 龌 龊 不 足 夸
past day foul not worth praise

jīn zhāo fàng dàng sī wú yá
今 朝 放 荡 思 无 涯
today unrestrained thoughts no border

chūn fēng dé yì mǎ tí jī
春 风 得 意 马 蹄 疾
spring wind very pleased horse shoe fast

yí rì kàn jìn cháng ān huā
一 日 看 尽 长 安 花
one day look exhaust Changan flower

孟 郊

22

# Horse Poem

In the great desert, the sand is like snow
and the moon like a hook over Mount Yan.
When will a gold halter rein my head
and my gallops tread gold autumn?

by Li He (791–817, Tang dynasty)

mǎ shī
马 诗
horse poem

dà mò shā rú xuě
大 漠 沙 如 雪
huge desert sand like snow

yān shān yuè sì gōu
燕 山 月 似 钩
Yan Mountain moon like
hook

hé dāng jīn luò nǎo
何 当 金 络 脑
when can gold halter head

kuài zǒu tà jīn qiū
快 走 踏 金 秋
fast gallop tread gold
autumn

李 贺

Li He started to write when he was seven. According to legend, Li often went out on his pony and wrote about his feelings and thoughts. By sunset, he would have filled a bag with writings.

He should have been a candidate for the *jinshi* exam, but he chose not to apply, he claimed, out of respect for his father, whose name sounded the same as *jinshi*. Li, like all respectful Chinese sons, never addressed his father by his given name. Unwilling to pronounce the word *jinshi* in public, he gave up his chance to have an official job.

The great Gobi Desert and Mount Yan, in the north-western part of China, seemed terrifyingly romantic to the ancient Chinese. The poet here imagined himself as a fine horse, eager to serve the emperor. He died of illness at age 26, and never had a chance to obtain an important position or fight for his country.

23

# I See the Signatures of Those Who Passed

## While Visiting the South Hall of Chong Zheng Temple

In radiant spring sun, cloudy peaks fill my eyes.
As it is born, each silver stroke of their words shines.
I hate my silk dress for hiding the poet inside
and raise my head in useless envy of the qualified.

by Yu Xuanji (844–868, Tang dynasty)

Although Yu Xuanji was born into a poor family, she became famous at 15 for improvising clever poems. Wen, a well-known poet, was so impressed that he volunteered to teach her.

One beautiful spring day, Yu and Wen visited a Daoist temple. A group of young men who had just passed the *jinshi* exam were writing poems on the temple wall, showing off their calligraphy. Yu watched with envy, and after they left, wrote this poem next to theirs.

While visiting Changan, a rich man, Li Yi, saw her poem. He asked Wen to introduce him to Yu, and immediately took her as his concubine. But his jealous wife was furious. Fearing her powerful family, Li left Yu in a Daoist temple and never returned. Yu wrote many poems to him, but had nowhere to send them. In despair, she became a Daoist priestess and made her living as a courtesan. Accused of killing her maid, she was executed. Her short and unhappy life depended on male support. When she lost it, she lost everything.

24

yóu chóng zhēn guàn nán lóu
游 崇 真 观 南 楼
visit Chong Zheng Temple south hall

dǔ xīn jí dì tí míng chù
睹 新 及 第 题 名 处
see new pass exam sign name place

yún fēng mǎn mù fàng chūn qíng
云 峰 满 目 放 春 晴
cloud peak fill eye radiant spring sunny

lì lì yíng gōu zhǐ xià shēng
历 历 银 钩 指 下 生
clearly every silver hook finger under born

zì hèn luó yī yǎn shī jù
自 恨 罗 衣 掩 诗 句
self hate silk dress hide poem sentence

jǔ tóu kōng xiàn bǎng zhōng míng
举 头 空 羡 榜 中 名
raise head vain envy list middle name

鱼 玄 机

# On Failing the Jinshi Exam

## Chrysanthemum Song

Just wait until the autumn chill arrives.
When hundreds lose their lives, I'll bloom and thrive.
Filling elegant Changan with my troops
armed in gold, my scent will soar to the sky!

by HUANG CHAO (?–884, Tang dynasty)

bú dì hòu fù jú
不 第 后 赋 菊
not passing exam chant
chrysanthemum

dài dào qiū lái jiǔ yuè bā
待 到 秋 来 九 月 八
wait till autumn come
ninth month eight

wǒ huā kāi guò bǎi huā shā
我 花 开 过 百 花 杀
my flower bloom after
hundred flower kill

chōng tiān xiāng zhèn xiù
cháng ān
冲 天 香 阵 秀 长 安
soaring sky fragrance
array elegant Changan

mǎn chéng jìn dài huáng jīn
jiǎ
满 城 尽 带 黄 金 甲
fill city all wear yellow
gold armor.

黄 巢

Huang Chao, an ambitious son of a rich merchant, decided not to retake the *jinshi* exam after he failed. He felt the corrupt regime was not worth serving, and joined a peasant rebellion.

Huang, whose family name means yellow in Chinese, is comparing himself with the chrysanthemum, the last flower that blooms before the winter arrives. The most common type is brilliant yellow and very fragrant. Born like the flower, in an unfavorable time, the poet intends to survive and triumph.

When his army grew strong, he came back to Changan, and did what his poem promised. His troops marched in shiny armor, thrusting their swords and shooting arrows high. The emperor fled.

Huang was killed after his brief success, but a rumor spread that he had somehow escaped. Some claimed to have seen his portrait and poems on a temple wall many years later.

# Painting a Rooster

You don't need a tailor to make his red crown
or his body parading snow-white down.
He doesn't dare to speak carelessly,
for with one crow, he can wake a whole town.

by TANG YIN (1470–1523, Ming dynasty)

huà jī
画 鸡
paint rooster

tóu shàng hóng guān bú yòng cái
头 上 红 冠 不 用 裁
head on red crown not need tailoring

mǎn shēn xuě bái zǒu jiāng lái
满 身 雪 白 走 将 来
whole body snow white walk majestically here

píng shēng bù gǎn qīng yán yǔ
平 生 不 敢 轻 言 语
all life not dare carelessly talk speak

yí jiào qiān hù wàn hù kāi
一 叫 千 户 万 户 开
one crow thousand door ten thousand door open

唐 寅

Everyone had high expectations for Tang Yin when, at 29, he ranked number one in a regional exam for government posts. His father had come from a family of high officials, but had been reduced to keeping a store. Tang's parents hoped he would pass the *jinshi* exam and restore his family's glory. Unfortunately, a friend bribed one of the judges to get the theme for the essay. Tang was accused of preparing essays for his friend and himself in advance. Both were jailed.

Tang's wife left him. His family was in disgrace. Forbidden to take the exam again, Tang lived in poverty. However, he did become a great painter and calligrapher. He probably wrote this poem on one of his paintings.

*Thousand doors* and *ten thousand doors* are parallel to each other, giving the poem a rhythm and a sense of balance.

## Song of a Traveling Son

yóu zǐ yín
游 子 吟
traveling son chant

cí mǔ shǒu zhōng xiàn
慈 母 手 中 线
kind mother hand inside
thread

yóu zǐ shēn shàng yī
游 子 身 上 衣
traveling son body upon
clothes

lín xíng mì mì féng
临 行 密 密 缝
before leave closely
closely stitch

yì kǒng chí chí guī
意 恐 迟 迟 归
feel afraid late late return

shuí yán cùn cǎo xīn
谁 言 寸 草 心
who say inch grass heart

bào dé sān chūn huī
报 得 三 春 晖
thank enough three
springs' sunshine

孟 郊

Thread from a mother's warm hand
travels on the back of her son.
Close, close stitches, before he leaves,
won't keep out fear for a latecoming one.
Does the heart of grass just one inch tall
know how to thank spring's nourishing sun?

by MENG JIAO (751–814, Tang dynasty)

Caring for aging parents was a son's duty. Leaving home, even to serve his emperor, was never a man's top choice as long as his parents were alive. He would be considered ungrateful to the people who gave him life. Also, travel was dangerous. A son who left home might never be seen again.

In this poem, a mother stitches her worries and love into her traveling son's clothing. Warm clothes might protect him from the weather, but not disease or bandits. The son feels guilty, knowing he can never pay back what he owes.

For centuries, this poem has been used to teach Chinese children to be grateful for their mothers' love and care. The spring sun symbolizes a nourishing mother and the inch-tall grass, the son. A Chinese spring is divided into early, middle, and late spring—the *three springs.*

# Remembering My Brothers

A stranger in a distant town, I ache to see
my family, and doubly on a holiday.
Far away, my brothers are trooping up a peak,
all wearing fragrant blooms, but missing me.

by WANG WEI (701–761, Tang dynasty)

Wang Wei, who passed the *jinshi* exam at 21, served at court, and was admired for his painting as well as his poetry.

In ancient times, the ninth day of the ninth month was an important holiday, *Chong Yang*. Families and friends would climb to high hilltops and wear fragrant blooms to ward off evil. This custom originated because of a legend:

A man named Huan Jin was warned by a Daoist priest, Zhang Fang, "Beware of the ninth day of the ninth month. Something disastrous is on its way. Tell your whole family to make embroidered pouches filled with *zhu yu* plants. Tie the pouches to your arms, then climb to a high place and drink chrysanthemum wine."

Huan Jin did what he was told. After the family returned home from the hills, they were astonished to see that all their chickens, dogs, cows, and sheep were dead. They felt lucky that they were not home when disaster struck.

Even today, the second line of the original poem is often recited on holidays. It sums up the feelings of Chinese who, like scholar-officials of old, have to leave their homeland and families behind.

jiǔ yuè jiǔ rì yì shān dōng xiōng dì
九月九日忆山东兄弟
ninth month ninth day recall mountain east brothers

dú zài yì xiāng wéi yì kè
独在异乡为异客
alone in foreign village as foreign guest

měi féng jiā jié bèi sī qīn
每逢佳节倍思亲
whenever encounter nice holiday doubly miss relative

yáo zhī xiōng dì dēng gāo chù
遥知兄弟登高处
distance imagine brothers climb high place

biàn chā zhū yú shǎo yì rén
遍插茱萸少一人
everywhere insert *zhu yu* miss one person

王维

# Bamboo Rock

zhú shí
竹 石
bamboo rock

yǎo dìng qīng shān bú fàng
sōng
咬 定 青 山 不 放 松
bite hold green mountain
not let loose

lì gēn yuán zài pò yán
zhōng
立 根 原 在 破 岩 中
set root actually in broken
rock middle

qiān mó wàn jī huán jiān jìn
千 磨 万 击 还 坚 劲
thousand grind ten
thousand attack still
strong vigorous

rèn ěr dōng xī nán běi fēng
任 尔 东 西 南 北 风
let you east west south
north wind

郑 板 桥

I bite and hold green mountains, not letting go.
In the middle of broken rock, I set my roots
    and grow.
Grind me down or beat me, I'm still tough
    and strong,
no matter how east, west, south, or north
    winds blow!

by Zheng Banqiao (1693–1765, Qing dynasty)

Zheng Banqiao, who was born into a very poor but literate family, took the *jinshi* exam many times. He finally passed it at age 44 and obtained a small post. Unlike his predecessors, he cared very much about the people. Without permission, he opened the government granary to the victims of a severe flood, and forced the rich to donate money to pay the flood victims to work on government projects. He made so many powerful enemies that he was forced out of office when he was 61. He retired into a world of painting and calligraphy. His paintings of bamboo were so free in spirit that his style is still copied.

Bamboo grows throughout much of China. Its stems are used to make furniture, buckets, poles, and pipes. The young shoots are served as food. Bamboo leaves can be used for roofs and raincoats. Chinese also love its shape and use its patterns for decoration. A hardy and simple plant, bamboo symbolizes the humble, yet vigorous. The poet suggests that he's like bamboo, not letting political enemies vanquish him.

# River Snow

Over a thousand mountains, no birds have flown
and ten thousand paths have lost all human tracks.
On a lone boat, an old man in straw cloak and hat
fishes on a snowy river, all alone.

by LIU ZONGYUAN (773–819, Tang dynasty)

Liu Zongyuan, born and raised in Changan, spent most of his life in exile after his chief supporter, a very high official, fell into disgrace. Liu was given only minor posts in remote areas. There he composed most of his poetry.

In this poem, he seems to portray himself as a lone fisherman, worthy but unappreciated. A legend that may have inspired the poet tells of a hermit, Jiang Taigong, who spent most of his time fishing with a straightened hook. When asked how he could catch a fish like this, he replied, "A willing soul will bite." The word reached his king, who understood: A willing ruler would listen to his most humble subjects. Jiang was invited to serve in the king's court. But the poet Liu was not as lucky.

Parallelism is a method widely used in Chinese poetry in which nouns, verbs, and adjectives match each other in successive lines. Parallelism is used throughout the poem and gives it an exceptional beauty and simplicity in Chinese.

jiāng xuě
江 雪
river snow

qiān shān niǎo fēi jué
千 山 鸟 飞 绝
thousand mountain bird
fly none

wàn jìng rén zōng miè
万 径 人 踪 灭
ten thousand path people
trace vanish

gū zhōu suō lì wēng
孤 舟 蓑 笠 翁
lonely craft reed-cloak
straw-hat old-man,

dú diào hán jiāng xuě
独 钓 寒 江 雪
alone fish cold river snow

柳 宗 元

# Leaving Baidi City in the Morning

Wrapped in morning's rosy clouds, Baidi, good-bye.
A thousand *li* in a day, back to Jiangling I glide.
From both river banks, gibbons howl on and on
as we pass ten thousand layered peaks, my boat and I.

by LI BAI (701–762, Tang dynasty)

zhǎo fā bái dì chéng
早 发 白 帝 城
morning leave Baidi
city

zhāo cí bái dì cǎi yún jiān
朝 辞 白 帝 彩 云 间
morning farewell Baidi
rosy cloud among

qiān lǐ jiāng líng yí rì huán
千 里 江 陵 一 日 还
thousand *Li* Jiangling one
day return

liǎng àn yuán shēng tí bú
zhù
两 岸 猿 声 啼 不 住
two bank gibbon sound
howl not stop

qīng zhōu yǐ guò wàn chóng
shān
轻 舟 已 过 万 重 山
light boat already pass ten
thousand layer mountain

李 白

Li Bai wasn't interested in the *jinshi* exam. He preferred to write and drink with his poet friends. They thought he was so talented that they recommended him to the emperor, Xuan Zong.

One day, when the peonies were in bloom, the emperor decided to celebrate. Instead of having a court singer singing the same old words to his favorite imperial concubine, Yang Yuhuan, the emperor called for new words from a celebrated poet. His men found Li Bai and brought him to the palace, drunk, as usual. Li Bai lay down and asked the head servant to take off his dirty boots. Then he asked Yang to prepare ink and hold the paper. She was not happy, and even less so when he mocked her in his poems. He compared her to concubines of the past who had fallen into disgrace. The emperor, who admired Li's talent, didn't punish him.

But Li's patron later rebelled against the emperor and Li was sent into exile. Later, when word reached him in Baidi that he was pardoned, he celebrated his freedom by boating down the wild gorges of the Yangzi River.

# In the Emerald Willows

Two orioles chirp in the emerald willows
and a line of white egrets flies up the blue sky.
Centuries of West Ridge snow fill my windows.
At my door, boats from far East Wu are tied.

by Du Fu (712–770, Tang dynasty)

Du Fu, today one of the most celebrated poets of the Tang dynasty, was dogged by misfortune all his life. He failed the *jinshi* exam more than once, but eventually the emperor read his writing and called him to serve in the court. Unfortunately, the emperor was driven out that very year (755).

Du Fu had such a high opinion of his own poetry that he prescribed it as a cure for malarial fever. Yet he thought he was a failure, in spite of his huge output, because he didn't live up to the Confucian ideal of public service.

In his time, wars erupted all over the country. Poverty, poor health, and family separation became frequent subjects. This poem, however, is an exception. The scene he described over a thousand years ago is full of color and life. Parallelism makes it especially harmonious in Chinese.

This poem has no title. Compilers of poetry collections called it *jueju*, a particular style of *shi* poem. We added the title "In the Emerald Willows."

jué jù
绝 句
ruled *shi* poem

liǎng gè huáng lì míng cuì liǔ
两 个 黄 鹂 鸣 翠 柳
two individual yellow oriole chirp emerald willow

yì háng bái lù shàng qīng tiān
一 行 白 鹭 上 青 天
one line white egret up blue sky

chuāng hán xī lǐng qiān qiū xuě
窗 含 西 岭 千 秋 雪
window hold West Ridge thousand autumn's snow

mén bó dōng wú wàn lǐ chuán
门 泊 东 吴 万 里 船
door anchor East Wu ten thousand li boat

杜 甫

# Song of a Well in a Small Yard

yǒng tiān jǐng
咏 天 井
song enclosed yard

tiān jǐn sì sì fāng
天 井 四 四 方
enclosed yard four side square

zhōu wéi shì gāo qiáng
周 围 是 高 墙
surround is high wall

qīng qīng xiàn luǎn shí
清 清 见 卵 石
clear clear show round pebble

xiǎo yú yǒu zhōng yāng
小 鱼 圈 中 央
little fish confine middle center

zhǐ hē jǐng lǐ shuǐ
只 喝 井 里 水
only drink well inside water

yóng yuǎn yǎng bù cháng
永 远 养 不 长
forever grow not long

毛 泽 东

A well sits in a small yard,

four high walls around it wrapped.

Through clear water pebbles show,

little fish inside it trapped.

If they drink just from this well,

they will never ever grow.

by MAO ZEDONG (1893–1976)

Mao Zedong was born into a prosperous peasant family in Hunan province. When he was 12, the teacher at his village school told the children to stay inside and study while he was away. After the teacher left, so did Mao. When Mao returned with chestnuts to share, his teacher demanded an explanation. Mao retorted, "You shut us up in this stuffy room. Even if we memorize all the sages' words, what good will it do?"

The angry teacher dragged Mao to a courtyard with a well in the middle. "Now, write a poem about this well or you will be spanked." Mao saw fish that children had set loose in the well and wrote this poem.

When Mao grew older, he left his mountain village. China was in great turmoil. The last dynasty, Qing, had ended, and with it the *jinshi* system. Warlords fought over territory. Foreign countries claimed parts of China. Educated Chinese struggled to bring in modern ideas and political systems.

In the 1920s, Mao joined the Chinese Communist Party and soon became its leader. After years of war, the Chinese communists defeated their nationalist opponents and established today's People's Republic of China in 1949.

Mao invited his old teacher to the capital, Beijing, and asked him how he'd liked the chestnuts. The teacher had forgotten the chestnuts, but remembered the poem.

# A Thousand Peaks

## Embracing Nature

MANY POET-OFFICIALS BECAME TIRED OF POLITICAL STRUGGLES. It seemed better, while dynasties were changing, or when an emperor was worthless, to leave the cities, living freely instead of serving. Poets were enraptured by China's mountains with their Daoist and Buddhist shrines and temples, by wild rivers and simple farming villages.

The philosophy of Daoism comes from the teachings of Lao Zi. Like Confucius, Lao Zi (whose name means Old Master) was a scholar-teacher who lived in the sixth century, B.C.E. But he was interested in encouraging people to live in harmony with nature, not society. Lao Zi believed that all things should be left to take their natural course. "Do nothing and all things will be done," Lao Zi said.

Daoists felt that the burden of a post and conspiracies in the court corrupted one's health and soul. It was best to live in peace with the universe, comfortable with the essential mystery at the root of all things. What difference did it make if one was climbing up or going down the shaky ladder of success? It was better to stand with both feet planted firmly on the ground.

The highest Daoist ideal was to reach immortality through contemplation, though some priests supplemented this with roots, herbs, and chemicals. These priests became the earliest chemists and doctors, trying to discover the elixir of life. Han Wudi, a Han emperor, asked a Daoist priest to brew him such a potion. The emperor's minister grabbed the potion and drank it himself. Furious, the emperor called for the death of his minister. "If the potion is real," the minister said, "you can't kill me. If it isn't, what harm has been done?" His reply saved his life.

Buddhism arrived from India in the first century C.E. The Indian prince, Gautama, was born around the same time as Confucius. He gave up all his possessions, lived as a wanderer, and freed himself from worldly ambitions, becoming the Buddha, the Enlightened One.

Buddhists believed behavior in this life would affect your position in the next. Buddhist monks and nuns were celibate, unlike Daoist priests and priestesses. Their heads were shaved, while Daoists had long, flowing hair. Both groups believed in meditation and the serenity that comes from contemplating nature, and were noted for their poetry.

The tradition of meditation made the Chinese keen observers. Poets, often artists themselves, liked to inscribe poems on paintings that were often mounted on long silk scrolls. Unwinding one, a viewer watched the panoramic landscape unroll like a moving picture. The poem, in a handsome calligraphy, narrated the thoughts and feelings behind the picture. The Song poet Su Shi, a celebrated painter and calligrapher, praised the Tang poet Wang Wei's paintings: "In his poetry there is painting and in his painting, poetry." Later poets continued to fuse the three great arts of painting, poetry, and calligraphy.

Many poets spent their lives torn between the Confucian and Daoist ideals. When they received an emperor's favor, they devoted their talents to serving the court and society. When they were out of favor or exiled, they followed Lao Zi's *dao*, or way, wandering in the wilderness.

# Storm at Lakeview Tower

Splattering mountains, ink-black clouds sweep by.
Bouncing on boats, pearl white raindrops fly.
Rolling around the earth, wind scatters clouds
until, under Lakeview Tower, water is sky.

by Su Shi (1036–1101, Song dynasty)

In the first century of the Song dynasty, agricultural production increased substantially, thanks to better irrigation and flood control. The population doubled. Still, the peasants were oppressed, heavily taxed and poor, and there were major revolts. Wanting to prevent unrest, the emperor Sheng Zong lowered taxes and introduced price controls. When his premier, Wang Anshi, carried out this reform, many landlords, officials, and merchants opposed it. Su Shi said the plan was too radical, and refused to support it.

He was demoted several times, as punishment. After Sheng Zong died, his son, Zhe Zong, slowly repealed his father's changes. The new court, dominated by conservative officials, called Su back to the capital and gave him an important post. Ironically, he did not want to abandon all Sheng Zong's reforms, and was again demoted. He was exiled at least 12 times.

Whenever he served in a provincial post, he had good relations with the common people. In Hangzhong, he organized a large water control project to irrigate the fields. He built a dike that still carries his name.

wàng hú lóu
望 湖 楼
Watch Lake Tower

hēi yún fān mò wèi zhē shān
黑 云 翻 墨 未 遮 山
black cloud splatter ink
not cover mountain

bái yǔ tiào zhū luàn rù chuán
白 雨 跳 珠 乱 入 船
white rain jump pearl
scatter into boat

juǎn dì fēng lái hū chuī sàn
卷 地 风 来 忽 吹 散
roll earth wind come
suddenly blow scatter

wàng hú lóu xià shuǐ rú tiān
望 湖 楼 下 水 如 天
Watch Lake Tower underneath water resemble sky

苏 轼

# White Gibbons in Autumn Cove

Autumn Cove is full of white gibbons.
Like flying snow, they leap and swoop.
They guide their young down from branches
to drink and play with the watery moon.

by LI BAI (701–762, Tang dynasty)

qiū pǔ qí wǔ
秋 浦 其 五
Autumn Cove poem
five

qiū pǔ duō bái yuán
秋 浦 多 白 猿
Autumn Cove many white
gibbon

chāo téng ruò fēi xuě
超 腾 若 飞 雪
superb prance like flying
snow

qiān yǐn tiáo shàng ér
牵 引 条 上 儿
draw guide branch on
children

yǐn nòng shuǐ zhōng yuè
饮 弄 水 中 月
drink play water middle
moon

李 白

Li Bai, his friend Du Fu, and Bai Juyi, are the best known of the Tang poets. Most experts agree that these three men brought poetry in the *shi* form to its highest level.

Li was not concerned with wealth and fame, but looked for adventure in the natural world. He grew up in Sichuan province, among high mountains and rocky cliffs. The Yangzi River cut through the mountains, creating dangerous gorges and nurturing wildlife. This natural barrier protected the people of Sichuan from invaders from the northern plains.

Li Bai wandered in the gorges and forests, often drinking and dancing with his sword. He was an excellent swordsman. One can easily imagine him swinging from trees and howling with the gibbons in his poem.

The moon was one of his favorite subjects. Some say Li died while trying to embrace the moon's reflection in the water. It's quite likely he was drunk!

# Watching Lushan Waterfall

From a sunlit Incense Burner, purple smoke grows
as flying down three thousand feet, the water goes.
Far away, I watch the falls hang over the river.
Can it be from highest heaven the Milky Way flows?

by LI BAI (701–762, Tang dynasty)

Lushan is a beautiful mountain range south of the Yangzi in today's Jiangxi province. It has been a Buddhist center since the Han dynasty. It was also a popular place for poets to visit, and many wrote poems about it.

*Incense Burner*, the name of the peak where the waterfall flows, also describes the misty appearance of the falls.

*Silver River* is the Chinese term for the Milky Way.

*Ninth Heaven* is the highest layer of heaven in the sky.

The second and fourth lines in the original poem share the same subject, the poet, who watches the waterfall and imagines seeing the Milky Way falling from the sky. Since English requires a stronger grammatical connection, the second and third lines are switched in the translation.

wàng lú shān pù bù
望 庐 山 瀑 布
watch Lushan water fall

rì zhào xiāng lú shēng zǐ yān
日 照 香 炉 生 紫 烟
sun light Incense Burner grow purple smoke

yáo kàn pù bù guà qián chuān
遥 看 瀑 布 挂 前 川
distance watch waterfall hang front river

fēi liú zhí xià sān qiān chǐ
飞 流 直 下 三 千 尺
fly water straight down three thousand feet

yí shì yín hé luò jiǔ tiān
疑 是 银 河 落 九 天
suspect is Silver River fall Ninth Heaven

李 白

# Lodging in the Monk's Hut

## In Sweet Dew Temple

Clouds drift inside my pillow on the air of a thousand peaks.

Under my bed, pines moan as if ten thousand chasms sigh.

To see sky-high waves lap a silver mountain,

I open the window and let the great river by.

by Zeng Gongliang (998–1078, Song dynasty)

sù gān lù sì sēng shè
宿 甘 露 寺 僧 舍
lodge Sweet Dew
Temple monk hut

zhěn zhōng yún qì qiān fēng jìn
枕 中 云 气 千 峰 近
pillow inside cloud air
thousand peak near

chuáng dǐ sōng shēng wàn hè āi
床 底 松 声 万 壑 哀
bed underneath pine
sound ten-thousand
chasm sad

yào kàn yín shān pāi tiān làng
要 看 银 山 拍 天 浪
want see silver mountain
lap sky wave

kāi chuāng fàng rù dà jiāng lái
开 窗 放 入 大 江 来
open window let in great
river come

曾 公 亮

In China, many temples are located in remote, beautiful places because the monks believed that nature could bring them closer to the gods. Temples were the only spacious buildings in those areas, and served as lodges for travelers and worshippers.

The temple in this poem was located near the river Zheng in Jiangsu province. Although there were no mountains or chasms nearby, the sound of the river made the poet imagine them.

Parallelism is obvious in the first two lines. The phrases match perfectly to create the parallel music of word and image.

# Willow Song

From the clear green jade of one tall tree,
ten thousand green ribbons hang silkily.
No one knows who cut out the thin leaves;
perhaps the wind-scissors of February.

by HE ZHIZHANG (659–744, Tang dynasty)

A famous poet in his time, when He Zhizhang became old, he asked to be excused from his government position. He spent the rest of his life living like a Daoist.

The willow tree is a symbol of hardiness, friendship, beauty, and sadness. Willows grow quickly and easily along rivers and lakes. The broken branches that fall into water sprout roots. Wherever a branch finds a suitable location, a new willow grows. Sometimes willows even grow between rocks in a swift stream. It was a custom in ancient China to give a traveling friend a willow branch. The friend would plant the willow when he reached his destination, and the tree would remind him of his past.

This poem is a classic seven-character-per-line *shi*. The first two lines describe the tree, the next poses a question, and the last gives an answer.

yǒng liǔ
咏 柳
chant willow

bì yù zhuāng chéng yí shù gāo
碧 玉 装 成 一 树 高
emerald jade put together one tree tall

wàn qiān chuí xià lǜ sī tāo
万 千 垂 下 绿 丝 绦
ten thousand thousand hang down green silk ribbon

bù zhī xì yè shuí cái chū
不 知 细 叶 谁 裁 出
not know thin leaf who cut out

èr yuè chūn fēng sì jiǎn dāo
二 月 春 风 似 剪 刀
second month spring wind like scissors

贺 之 章

40

# Spring Snow

The New Year has brought no fragrant blossoms.
Grass shoots are the second month's first surprise.
Disliking the delay of spring colors,
through courtyard trees, like flowers, white snow flies.

by HAN YU (768–824, Tang dynasty)

chūn xuě
春雪
spring snow

xīn nián dōu wèi yǒu fāng
huá
新 年 都 未 有 芳 华
New Year already not has
fragrant flower

èr yuè chū jīng jiàn cǎo yá
二 月 初 惊 见 草 芽
second month first
surprise see grass shoot

bái xuě què xián chūn sè
wǎn
白 雪 却 嫌 春 色 晚
white snow however
dislike spring color late

gù chuān tíng shù zuò fēi
huā
故 穿 庭 树 作 飞 花
deliberately pass court-
yard tree as flying flower

韩 愈

Han Yu was a scholar, writer, and teacher. After he passed
the *jinshi* exam at age 24, he held various posts, including
that of professor at the Imperial University. He was exiled
and recalled to the court several times, punished for being
outspoken, especially for criticizing the emperor's devo-
tion to Buddhism. He grew old prematurely, became ill,
and died in Changan, at the height of his success.

The houses of most prosperous Chinese were built
around one or more courtyards. All the rooms faced the
courtyard, which provided light and fresh air. Courtyards
were often landscaped with trees and plants. A large sturdy
front gate opened to the street. This design enabled families
to share their lives and protected the house from intruders.

# Flower Shadows

One on top of the other, up jade steps they creep.

I called the houseboy, but he failed to sweep

away what the sun soon cleaned,

and then the bright moon piled them deep.

by Su Shi (1037–1101, Song dynasty)

Su Shi was not only a great poet and painter, but a celebrated prose writer and calligrapher. Most critics consider him the greatest poet of the Song dynasty.

The Song was an artistic, refined era. Its emperors preferred collecting paintings, books, and fine pottery to fighting nomadic invaders from the north. After Su Shi's time, the court was forced to flee south. There, the luxurious court life continued until Genghis Khan's grandson, Kublai Khan, invaded. The Song dynasty was over and Beijing became the capital of the new Chinese/Mongolian empire.

Parallelism is used in the third and fourth lines. The phrases *sun clean up* and *moon sent back* give the celestial bodies a human character.

huā yǐng
花 影
flower shadow

chóng chóng dié dié shàng yáo tái
重 重 迭 迭 上 瑶 台
Overlap overlap pile pile up jade step

jǐ dù hū tóng sǎo bù kāi
几 度 呼 童 扫 不 开
several time call houseboy sweep not away

gāng bèi tài yáng shōu shí qù
刚 被 太 阳 收 拾 去
Just let sun clean up away

què jiào míng yuè sòng jiāng lái
却 叫 明 月 送 将 来
but let bright moon send back over

苏 轼

# The Freezing Fly

Outside my window, a fly bathed in sun,
rubbing two feet to play with the warmth.
Sensing sun and shadows about to move,
to another window it whisked its song.

by YANG WANLI (1124–1206, Song dynasty)

dòng yíng
冻 蝇
freezing fly

gé chuāng ǒu jiàn fù xuān yíng
隔 窗 偶 见 负 暄 蝇
outside window once see
carry sun fly

shuāng jiǎo ruó suō nòng
xiǎo qíng
双 脚 接 挱 弄 晓 晴
two feet rub play morning
sunny

rì yǐng yù yí xiān huì dé
日 影 欲 移 先 会 得
sun shadow about move
advance know already

hū rān fēi luò bié chuāng
shēng
忽 然 飞 落 别 窗 声
suddenly fly down other
window sound

杨 万 里

Yang Wanli was a *jinshi* scholar who served four genera-
tions of Song emperors. He wouldn't do anything against
his principles. He once refused to help a powerful official
write an essay because he thought he was corrupt. He said
he'd rather quit his job.

Poets in Yang's day relished topics, such as lice or flies,
which the Tang poets had shunned. Yang and his fellow
poets did not want to imitate great writers who came be-
fore them. They enjoyed the challenge of making beauty
out of what was usually considered ugly. Many of Yang's
poems have humble subjects, but his keen observations and
touching descriptions of the physical world give them a
surprising beauty.

Perhaps Yang was comparing this fly with a politician
who didn't act on his beliefs, but flew to whoever would
benefit him.

# Song of the Geese

Geese, geese, geese,

curved necks singing to the sky.

They float on green, feathery white,

red feet stirring waves of light.

by Luo Binwang (Tang dynasty)

Composed by Luo when he was only seven, this poem is often included in textbooks for children because it is simple and easy to memorize. The characters are also commonly used words.

Luo Binwang became an adult at a time when China was ruled by the woman emperor, Wu Zetian. She called herself Son of Heaven. Luo believed it was against the will of heaven to let a woman rule, so he helped a friend, Xu Jinye, write a declaration giving reasons to depose her. The empress was very impressed by his writing and complained, "How come my premier didn't get him to serve me?" But Xu failed to get Wu deposed, and Luo fled.

The third and the fourth lines of this poem use parallelism, with matching adjectives, verbs, and nouns forming a couplet. Notice in the original poem how *white feather* and *red feet* are parallel adjectives with nouns, *float* and *stir* are parallel verbs, and *green water* and *clear wave* are parallel adjectives with nouns.

yǒng é
咏 鹅
chant goose

é é é
鹅 鹅 鹅
goose goose goose

qǔ xiàng xiàng tiān gē
曲 项 向 天 歌
curve neck towards sky sing

bái máo fú lǜ shuǐ
白 毛 浮 绿 水
white feather float green water

hóng zhǎng bō qīng bō
红 掌 拨 清 波
red feet stir clear wave

骆 宾 王

# *Wind*

It can make the leaves of late autumn fall
or spring flowers bloom, wherever it walks.
It can raise waves a thousand feet high
or slant ten thousand bamboo stalks.

by Li Qiao (644–715, Tang dynasty)

fēng
风
wind

jiě luò sān qiū yè
解 落 三 秋 叶
loosen fall third autumn's
leaf

néng kāi èr yuè huā
能 开 二 月 花
can bloom second month
flower

guò jiāng qiān chǐ làng
过 江 千 尺 浪
pass river thousand feet
wave

rù zhú wàn gān xié
入 竹 万 竿 斜
enter bamboo ten
thousand pole slanting

李峤

When Li Qiao was young, he dreamed that a spirit left him a pair of brushes. Many believed that those brushes symbolized his writing talent.

The Chinese tracked the seasons by the cycles of the moon. Since a Chinese New Year can be anytime in late January or early February, the *second month* can fall in late February or early March. We translated the *second month* in this poem as *spring* because the timing is not very clear.

The parallelism in this poem is very obvious. The third word in every line of the original poem is a number and the fourth a measuring unit.

# Grass on an Ancient Field

## A Farewell Song

The lushest field grass
in one year flourishes and dies,
but wild fires can't destroy
what spring winds blow alive.
Faraway scents invade old roads;
green touches towns left to die.
Waving farewell to travelers,
the thick grass quivers with good-byes.

by BAI JUYI (772–846, Tang dynasty)

Bai Juyi composed this poem at age 15. He was wildly popular in his lifetime, loved by royalty and common people alike, and his fame spread to Korea and Japan. He used common language in his poems, and often rewrote them so that the most uneducated listeners could understand. Traveling throughout China, he saw his poems copied on the walls of inns and monasteries.

In Chinese, the third and fourth lines of this poem use parallel phrases, *wild fire burn* and *spring wind blow,* to describe the vitality of the grass. The fifth and sixth lines are also parallel and give us the scent and the color of the thriving grass in a once civilized town. The first and last two lines enclose the poem in its theme: Though the grass dies once a year, it endures, a witness to the deepest human feelings.

The poem's first line has the double phrase *lush lush* and the last line *luxuriant luxuriant* to describe the grass.

fù dé gǔ yuán cǎo sòng bié
赋得古原草送别
compose ready ancient
field grass see off

lí lí yuán shàng cǎo
离离原上草
lush lush field top grass

yí suì yī kū róng
一岁一枯荣
one year one wither
flourish

yě huǒ shāo bú jìn
野火烧不尽
wild fire burn not extinct

chūn fēng chuī yòu shēng
春风吹又生
spring wind blow again
alive

yuǎn fāng qīn gǔ dào
远芳侵古道
distant fragrance invade
ancient road

qíng cuì jiē huāng chéng
晴翠接荒城
clear emerald touch
abandoned city

yòu sòng wáng sūn qù
又送王孙去
again see-off traveling
men leave

qī qī mǎn bié qíng
萋萋满别情
luxuriant luxuriant fill
parting feeling

白居易

# The Rosy Cloud

From dying sunlight, stroke by stroke, it grows
in layers, as if splitting shades of rose.
A heavenly wind cut it to pieces,
it seems, to make the fairies clothes.

by WANG ZHOU (Tang dynasty)

xiá
霞
rosy cloud

fú fú shēng cán huī
拂 拂 生 残 晖
stroke stroke grow dying sunlight

céng céng rú liè fēi
层 层 如 裂 绯
layer layer seem splitting crimson

tiān fēng jiǎn chéng piàn
天 风 剪 成 片
heavenly wind cut into piece

yí zuò xiān rén yī
疑 作 仙 人 衣
suspect for fairy clothes

王 周

At the beginning of the Tang dynasty, court scholars collected poems and documented the lives of many poets. At the end of the dynasty, a time of political unrest, this record-keeping was neglected. Perhaps that is why we know little about Wang Zhou, although he left us one volume of poems. Other poets may have been overlooked because they came from humble backgrounds.

The first two lines of this poem use parallelism to describe the clouds during a sunset. The third line gives a twist, leading to a fanciful conclusion. Double phrases are used in the first two lines to create balanced sounds and for emphasis.

# Climbing Stork Tower

White sun sets behind the mountain.
The Yellow River enters ocean.
If you want to stretch your eyes to explore
another thousand *li*, climb one story more.

by WANG ZHIHUAN (688–742, Tang dynasty)

dēng guàn què lóu
登 鹳 雀 楼
climb Stork Sparrow
Tower

bái rì yī shān jìn
白 日 依 山 尽
white sun by mountain set

huāng hé rù hǎi liú
黄 河 入 海 流
Yellow River enter ocean
current

yù qióng qiān lǐ mù
欲 穷 千 里 目
want extend thousand *li*
eye

gèng shàng yì céng lóu
更 上 一 层 楼
again up one story tower

王 之 涣

Stork Tower was a three-story building overlooking the Yellow River in Shanxi province in northwest China. According to legend, *guan que*, a type of stork, used to flock on the tower. The tower was so high that it seemed possible to see the end of the Yellow River over 1,000 *li* away. Three *li* equals about one mile.

This poem is often recited to encourage young people to try harder and achieve more in life. There is always more to see and more to read.

# Afterword

I first read some of these poems when I was 13. I was astonished to learn that such exquisite language existed.

I was two years old when China's Cultural Revolution began in 1966. For 10 years, fierce political struggles caused disruptions in every aspect of life. Both traditional and Western ideas were blamed for holding China back. Many books were banned for fear they would corrupt the people's revolutionary spirit.

My schoolbooks were filled with quotes and poetry from the writings of China's leader, Mao Zedong. Children were given so few books that I had read everything available by the time I was 10. One day I discovered a few books, yellowed with age, buried deep in my parents' closet. On one, in my mother's handwriting, was written "poisonous weed."

*Those must be the bad books published before the Cultural Revolution,* I thought. *Why didn't my parents burn them? Could we get into trouble?* Scared, I put them back.

One day, desperate for something to read, I opened one. *I am only trying to figure out what is so bad. I won't let it ruin me,* I reasoned.

Fear of punishment kept my lips sealed, but as I read I wondered, *What do fair maidens wear? What is the perfume of roses?* I was surrounded by people wearing only drab clothes. Our homes and surroundings were dreary and bare. *What is love between people?* I was expected to grow up to be an unemotional soldier, prepared to sacrifice myself for the great cause of our country and revolution.

After Mao Zedong died in 1976, the political climate changed, and books reappeared. Overjoyed, I read day and night. One of my favorites was *Three Hundred Poems of the Tang Dynasty*. I spent hours with my friends, reading and memorizing our favorites. I was angry that I had been fooled into believing that such books were bad for us.

Today I have two young daughters. Eager to share this rich heritage with them, I asked Orel Protopopescu, poet and children's author, to help me capture the spirit and meaning of these poems.

—*Siyu Liu*

I don't speak or read Chinese. How did I translate these poems? Siyu gave me prose translations and word-for-word transcriptions of the Chinese characters. I learned that some phrases could have several different meanings and tried to suggest them in my translations. Wherever possible, I matched rhyming lines, using precise or slant rhymes, metered or syllabic verse. My syllabic verses are less economical than the Chinese originals, because a Chinese character is always one syllable. Many translators render four-line poems into eight English lines. I wanted to keep the original structure and rhyme scheme, as much as possible without sounding forced.

The Chinese language has no plurals, articles, or inflected verbs, indicating tense. It can suggest so much in a few words, which makes it ideal for writing poetry. When I looked at other translations, I was fascinated by the different interpretations.

We selected our favorite poems from various Chinese-language sources. Some poems are well-known. Others were included to illuminate stories we wanted to tell. Our workshops on Chinese art and poetry for teachers and students helped us develop the book and its companion teacher's guide. We invite you to share our delight in the poems and the world that created them.

—*Orel Protopopescu*

# The Chinese Language:
## Its Pronunciation and Translation

Although Chinese can be written from top to bottom and right to left, we used the modern arrangement, which is the same as English. The phonetic transcription of the Mandarin pronunciation (based on the Beijing dialect) appears in the line above the characters and below appears its direct translation.

This book uses the *pinyin* system of phonetic transcription. Letters which are pronounced differently in English are listed below:

"a" as *a* in *father*

"o" as *ore* in *more*

"e" as *er* in *brother*

"u" as *oo* in *food*

"ü" is not present in English. It is like *u* pronounced with puckered lips,

"zh" as *j* in *jelly*

"c" as *ts* in *its*

"q" as *ch* in *chew*

"x" as *sh* in *sheet*

In general, each character has only one syllable. When you see *ai, ao,* or *ui*, etc., try to combine the two sounds into one. In addition, each character is pronounced with a specific tone. There are four tones, the first one is flat "−", the second rises "/", the third falls and then rises "v", and the fourth falls "\". Characters with the same romanization may mean different things.

The Chinese language has no plural, inflected verbs, indicating tense, or articles. A syllable may be read as a noun, verb, or adjective, or even have several functions at once.

While reading these poems in Chinese, you may notice that some of them do not rhyme at all. This may be because the pronunciation of characters has changed through the years; characters that used to rhyme do not anymore. It may also be because the poet spoke a dialect that sounded different from the standard.

## A Note on Illustration

The small, black and white illustrations are based on Chinese characters. Following are the English translations of the characters and their page numbers.

*Section One: Social Structure*

grain 10, palace 11, cloud 12, chrysanthemum 13, city 14, female 15, boil 16, flower 17, trunk 18, person 19

*Section Two: Scholar-Officials*

unrestrained 22, horse 23, clothes 24, armor 25, rooster 26, sew 27, alone 28, bamboo 29, old man 30, boat 31, willow 32, well 33

*Section Three: Embracing Nature*

rain 36, moon 37, river 38, peak and air 39, silk 40, snow 41, shadow 42, window 43, goose 44, wind 45, grass 46, crimson 47, sun, mountain, and current 48

# Resources for Teachers and Young Readers

## Poetry and Language

Lai, Him Mark, Genny Lim and Judy Yung. *Island: Poetry and History of Chinese Immigrants on Angel Island 1910–1940*, Seattle: University of Washington Press, 1991.

Goldstein, Peggy. *Long Is A Dragon: Chinese Writing for Children.* Berkeley: Pacific View Press, 1991.

Rexroth, Kenneth, and Ling Chung. *The Orchid Boat.* New York: McGraw–Hill, 1972.

Watson, Burton, ed. *The Columbia Book of Chinese Poetry.* New York: Columbia University Press, 1984.

## Chinese History

Allison, Amy. *Life in Ancient China.* San Diego: Lucent Books, 2000.

Chu, Daniel. *China.* New York: Scholastic, Inc., 1986.

Cotterell, Arthur. *Ancient China.* New York: Eyewitness Books, 1994.

Huntington, Madge. *A Traveler's Guide to Chinese History.* New York: Henry Holt, 1997.

Major, John S. *The Silk Route.* New York: HarperCollins, 1995.

Martell, Hazel Mary. *The Ancient Chinese.* New York: New Discovery Books, Macmillan Publishing, 1993.

Michaelson, Carol, ed. *Ancient China.* Sidney: Nature Company, 1996.

Millar, Heather. *China's Tang Dynasty.* Tarrytown, NY: Benchmark Books, 1996.

Stefoff, Rebecca. *China.* New York: Chelsea House, 1999.

Williams, Suzanne. *Made in China: Ideas and Inventions from Ancient China.* Berkeley: Pacific View Press, 1996.

## Chinese Philosophy

Mitchell, Stephen. *Tao Te Ching.* New York: Harper & Row, 1988.

## For Teachers

Liu, Siyu and Protopopescu, Orel. *A Thousand Peaks: A Teacher's Guide.* New York: Liu and Protopopescu, 2001.

Williams, Suzanne. *A Teacher's Guide to Made in China: Ideas and Inventions from Ancient China.* Berkeley: Pacific View Press, 1998.

# Index

Note: Chinese names are written with the surname first and given name second. The words in parentheses are translations of the names by other phonetic systems.